MY FIRST PAS WORDS PICTURE BOOK FOR KIDS

MW00887482

A Pashto picture language learning WORD study book with English translations for children aged 4 and above. This is a beautiful color picture book for children of ages 4+ and beginners to learn PASHTO and English everyday familiar words linked with it and its phonetics for simple comprehension and reference with pictures.

Marilyn Trueluck

Pashto Alphabets

ا, آ	ب	پ	ت	ټ	ث	ج	څ	چ	ځ	ح
خ	د	ډ	ذ	ر	ړ	ز	ژ	ږ	س	ش
ښ	ص	ض	ط	ظ	ع	غ	ف	ق	ك	ګ
ل	م	ن	ڼ	و	ه	ۀ	ي	ې	ی	ۍ
ئ										

Pashto contains 45 letters and four diacritics. The language is a version of the Perso-Arabic script and is usually written from right to left, the opposite of English. Pashto uses all 28 Arabic alphabet letters and has three letters in common with Persian and Urdu. Pashto has more vowels than Arabic and Persian; hence it has more characters that represent vowel sounds than the Perso-Arabic alphabet.

boy

هلک helk

girl

نجلى nejləi

man

سری sṛy

woman

ښبخه šch

father

پلار pelar

mother

مور mewr

brother

ورور werwer

sister

خور khewr

uncle

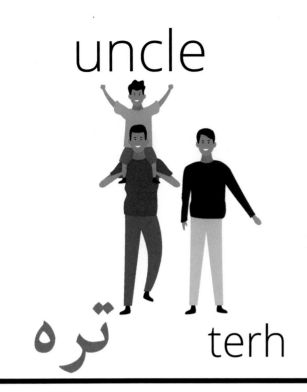

 تره

terh

aunt

ترور (خاله)

terwer (khalh)

bull

غويي

ghewyey

cow

غوا

ghewa

bathroom

تشناب

teshenab

bed

کت

kṭ

bedroom

دخوب خونه

dekhewb khewnh

chair

چوکی

chewkəi

clothes

جامی
jama

coat

کوت
kewṭ

cup

پیاله
paalh

desk

دفتری میز
deftera maz

dress

نبخَئينه جامى

šzanh jama

floor

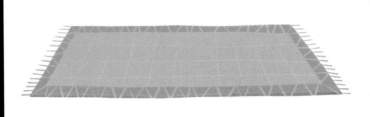

غولي

ghewley

fork

كاشوغ پنجه

kashewgh penjh

furniture

فرنيچر

fernacher

glass

كيلاس

galas

hat

خولى

khewla

house

كور

kewr

ink

رنګ

reng

jacket

جاکت

jakṭ

kitchen

اشپزخانه

ashepzekhanh

knife

چاره

charh

lamp

چراغ

cheragh

letter

لیك

leyk

map

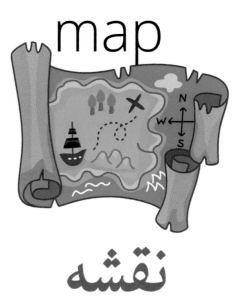

نقشه

neqshh

newspaper

ورځپاڼ

werzepaṇ

notebook

دیادانبت کتابچه

daadašt ketabechh

pants

پتلون

petlewn

paper

کاغذ

kaghez

pen

قلم

qelm

pencil

پنسل

pensel

picture

انځور

anezwer

plate

پشقاب

pesheqab

refrigerator

یخچال

yekhechal

restaurant

رستورانت

restewranet

car

موټر

moTar

rug

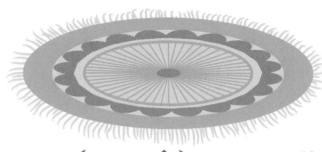

قالینه (غالی)

qalanh (ghala)

scissors

قیچي

qeychey

water

اوبه

Ooba

shirt

كميس

kemas

shoes

بوتان

bewṭan

soap

صابون

sabewn

socks

جرابى

jeraba

spoon

قاشوغه

qashewghh

table

میز (دسترخوان)

maz (desterkhewan)

toilet

تشناب

teshenab

toothbrush

دغا نبو برش

degha šw bersh

toothpaste

دغا ښو کريم

degha ṣ̌w keram

towel

ځان پاک

zan pak

umbrella

چتری

chetrəi

underwear

نيکر

naker

wall

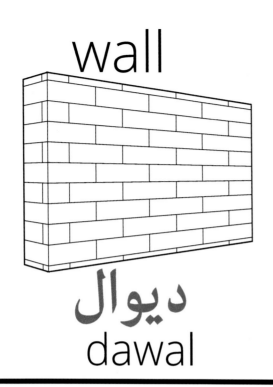

ديوال

dawal

wallet

بٹوہ

bṭwh

window

کھڑکی

kṛkəi

telephone

ٹیلی فون

ṭala fewn

arm

بازو (مت)

bazew (mṭ)

back

شا

sha

cheeks

غمبوری

ghembewra

chest

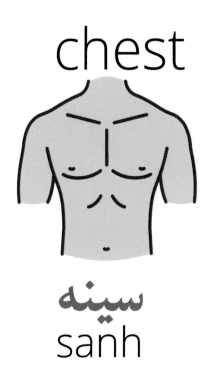

سینه

sanh

chin

زنه
zenh

ear

غوږ
g̈hewẓ̌

elbow

څنګل
cengel

eye

سترگه
setregh

face

مخ

mekh

fingers

ګوتى

gewta

heart

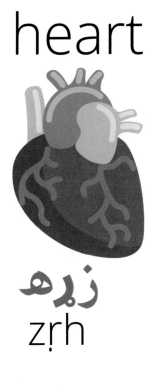

زړه

zṛh

foot

پنبه

pšh

hair

وینښتان

waṣ̌tan

hand

لاس

las

head

سر

ser

knee

زنګون

zengewn

stomach

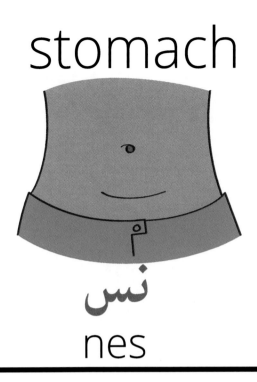

نس

nes

leg

پنښه

pṣ̌h

teeth

غاښوونه

ghaṣ̌wenh

mouth

خوله

khewlh

neck

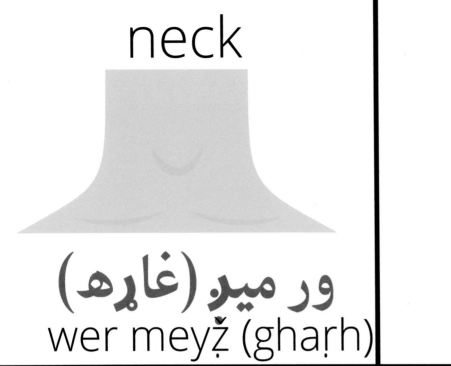

ور ميِژ (غاړه)

wer meyž (ghaṛh)

nose

پزه

pezh

thigh

ورون

werwen

tongue

ژبه

jebh

Monday

دوشنبه

dewshenbh

Tuesday

سه شنبه

sh shenbh

wednesday

چهار شنبه

chhar shenbh

thursday

پنج شنبه

penj shenbh

friday

جمعه
jem'eh

saturday

هفته
hefth

sunday

یک شنبه
ak shenbh

food

غذا
gheda

almonds

بادام

badam

bread

ḍوḍی

ḍwḍəi

breakfast

سبا ناری (دسحار چای)

seba nara (deshar chaa)

butter

کوچ

kewch

candy

شیرینی

sharana

cheese

پنیر

penyer

chicken

چرگ

cherg

tea

چای

Chaai

dessert

پودين

pewḍyen

cheese

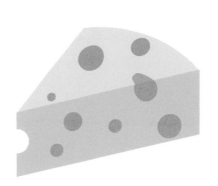

پنیر

penyer

dinner

دشپی دوډی

deshepa ḍwḍa

fish

ماهی (کب)

maha (keb)

fruit

مېوه

mewh

ice cream

ايسکريم

aasekram

lamb

د پسه غوښنبه

d pesh ghewṣh

lemon

لېمو

lemew

lunch

د غرمې ډوډۍ

d gherm̤ ḍwḍəi

meal

ډوډۍ

ḍwḍəi

meat

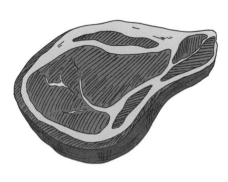

غوښه

ghewṣh

oven

تنور

tenwer

pepper

مرچ

merch

plants

نباتات

nebatat

pork

دخوک غوښه

dekhewg ghewṣh

salad

سلاته

selath

salt

مالګه

malegh

sand wich

سند ويچ
send wach

sausage

سپينکي

sepyenkey

soup

ښوروا

ṣwerwa

sugar

بوره

bewrh

turkey

فيلمرغ

falemregh

apple

منه

mṇh

banana

كيله

kalh

oranges

نارنج

narenj

peaches

شفتالو

sheftalew

peanut

پلی

pela

pears

ناک

nak

pineapple

اناناس

ananas

grapes

انگور

anegwer

strawberries

خُمكنيْ توتان

zemkeny tewtan

vegetables

سبزیجات

sebzajat

flowers

كلونه

gelwenh

football

فوټبال

fewṭbal

garden

بڼ

bṇ

moon

سپوږمی

sepwžməi

music

موسيقي

mewseyqey

tree

ونه

wenh

cold

يخ

akh

hot

گرم

germ

rain

باران

baran

snow

واوره

wawerh

baby

ماشوم

mashewm

grandfather

نیکه

neykh

nurse

نرس

ners

policeman

پولیس

pewleys

postman

پوسته رسان

pewseth resan

teacher

ښوونکي

ṣ̌wewneky

Made in the USA
Monee, IL
16 February 2024

53627008R00026